This book belongs to:

_____

My Grandma's Hands

Written by Susan Wardell   Illustrated by Katrina Smith

BEAVER'S
POND
PRESS

When I was born, **my** grandma's hands were some of the first to hold me. They held me close and welcomed me to the world.

When I was learning to walk, I sometimes would wobble and wobble and then fall.

Grandma took my hand and said, "Hold my hand. It is safer when we are together."

One time I was walking
on a dock and I nearly
fell in the water.

Guess whose hands caught me?

Later, when I was older, I learned to jump off that same dock into the water.

My grandma's hands caught me again and again and again!

My grandma loves to sing. Even if her voice sounds funny, I sing with her.

Her hands clap out the rhythm and we dance.

My grandma's hands often have a book in them. I sit on her lap and she lets me hold the book. I learn to turn the pages carefully.

As I get older and start learning to read, her finger points to the words as she helps me sound them out.

Later, I read to her!

My grandma's hands have lines, spots, and veins on them. I sit on her lap or at the table and play with them. I am fascinated by them.

She says they are old but I think they are interesting, as though they tell the story of her life.

"What is that on your hand?" I ask.
"That is a mother's ring," she answers. "It is one birthstone for each child I had, each one born in a different month." I count the stones—there are four of them! She shows me which one is my mom's birthstone.

The older I get, the bigger I grow. Soon my hands are bigger than **my** grandma's hands. I am too big to sit on my grandma's lap!

Whenever I play music, dance, or score the winning run, I can hear **my** grandma's hands clapping and her voice cheering in the crowd.

One day after a softball game, we had to walk a long way back to the parking lot.

As we got closer to the car I saw my grandma stumble. She nearly fell to the ground. Gently, I took her hand and said, "Hold **my** hand. It is safer when we are together."

To McKinley, who inspired me, to Doug,
who believed in me. To Marian Palmer, aka "Gommy,"
who had the best set of Grandma's hands, and to all the
Palmer grandchildren, who played with those hands!
And to K, L, C, and M—I love you! –SW

To my family, whose love and support
helped me to live my dream of becoming
a children's book illustrator.
To my puppy, Oliver, whose cuddles
are the best. –KS

Author

Susan Wardell is a mother of four children
and grandmother of three. A retired preschool
teacher, she has read hundreds of children's
books! She also taught special education for
several years in St. Paul, Minnesota. She lives
in northern Minnesota with her husband, Doug,
and their dog, Waylon. She loves to hike, bike,
stand-up paddleboard, and craves time with
her grandchildren. She's very proud to have
her own set of Grandma Hands.

Illustrator

Katrina Smith fell in love with illustrating
when it transported her from her struggles as
a deaf child to a vivid visual world of color. As
she makes adaptations to the hearing world
she still gravitates toward her childlike artist's
imagination. She studied art at Northwest
College, Savannah College of Art and Design,
and earned her bachelor of arts from the
University of Wyoming. Her nieces, nephews,
and beloved sheltie, Oliver, remind her to let
her inner child out to play!

Edited by Lily Coyle
Illustrated by Katrina Smith

ISBN: 978-1-59298-671-2
Library of Congress Catalog Number: 2018908330
Printed in the United States of America
First Printing: 2018
22 21 20 19 18   5 4 3 2 1

Cover and interior design by Sara J Weingartner

Beaver's Pond Press, Inc.
7108 Ohms Lane
Edina, MN 55439-2129

BEAVER'S
POND
PRESS

(952) 829-8818
www.BeaversPondPress.com

To order, visit www.ItascaBooks.com or call (952) 345-4488.
Reseller discounts available. SusanWardell.com